Yosemite
National Park

Yosemite evokes a sense of inspiration, wonder, and mystique. Some call it magical. The constant interplay of water, weather, and light on ts sublime scenery captures forms, textures, and colors of both breathtaking splendor and serene subtlety.

*B*eyond the placid Merced River,
its flow ebbing in late summer,
morning mist slowly releases
its grip on Leidig Meadow as sunlight
begins to bathe Yosemite Valley.

Yosemite National Park, located in central California, was established in 1890; it preserves Yosemite Valley, giant sequoias, other forests, and High Sierra wilderness.

Front cover: Yosemite Falls, photo by Gail Bandini. Inside front cover: Sentinel Rock in autumn, photo by Josef Muench. Page 1: Along Illilouette Creek; Pages 2/3: Early morning on the Merced River, photos by Dianne Dietrich Leis. Pages 4/5: Sawtooth Ridge, photo by Carr Clifton.

Edited by Cheri C. Madison.
Book design by K. C. DenDooven.

Eighth Printing, 2007 • New Version

in pictures YOSEMITE Nature's Continuing Story™
© 1991 KC PUBLICATIONS, INC.

"in pictures…The Continuing Story"; the Eagle / Flag icon on Front Cover are registered in the U.S. Patent and Trademark Office

LC 91-60042. ISBN 0-88714-057-2.

in pictures

Yosemite

Nature's Continuing Story™

by Leonard McKenzie

LEONARD MCKENZIE was Chief of Interpretation at Yosemite National Park from 1974 to 1993. With a biology degree from the University of New Mexico, Len has served in interpretive capacities with the National Park Service at several parks.

...the Story of Yosemite

PAT O'HARA

The concept of having National Parks, for everyone to see and enjoy, was pioneered by the Yosemite Grant signed by President Abraham Lincoln in 1864. Today this idea has flourished all over the world.

Yosemite National Park is a land of spectacular contrasts. A granite mountain sliced in half by a glacier. Vast expanses of terrain where virtually nothing grows, or so it would seem at first! And trees that are among the oldest and largest living things on earth. All of this can be seen at Yosemite in a single day – if one insists on traveling that fast.

Each distinct area of Yosemite is worth a separate vacation trip in itself, (now, isn't that a neat idea!) One can see nature up close and personal from tiny belly-button flowers to towering trees. Here, there are animals you would seldom see to chirping birds, welcoming you to their Park.

Take the time to see the total Yosemite. Whether on a family vacation or on a "must-get-away-from-it-all" per-sonal trip, this is a Park of great diversity. And yet most of it is available by getting out and hiking a trail or two, or more!

Yosemite was an important concept back in the mid 1800's. It was one of the key building blocks for establishing the entire National Park System. Today it is here for us to use, enjoy and appreciate.

Come see and enjoy Yosemite!

K.C. DenDooven
Publisher

The lower step in the Giant Stairway–cliffs quarried by glaciers that scooped out vertically jointed rock when they descended the Merced River canyon–Vernal Fall, 317 feet high and 80 feet wide at peak flow, attracts thousands of hikers each summer day.

...an epic adventure of life and death.

FRED HIRSCHMANN

FRANK S. BALTHIS

Thick, spongy bark and tannin-rich wood retard burning, enabling sequoias to survive most fires. This furrowed pillar towers over the Mariposa Grove Museum, the site where Galen Clark, first guardian of the Yosemite Grant, built a cabin in the early 1860s. Clark first brought public attention to the grove, here mantled by fresh snow that enhances the trees' stately nobility.

Wilderness offers backpackers solitude and spiritual refreshment–the "tonic" of wild places. Where heavy use ruts a trail, hikers often walk alongside the route, ultimately creating parallel paths. The scars may require decades to heal, for the growing season is short.

Yosemite: the Valley—Water: the Force

Anthropologist Loren Eiseley wrote, "If there is magic on this planet, it is contained in water." The lifeblood of any biological system as well as a powerful cutting force, water transforms landscapes and sustains all life on and in them. Perhaps it is water, more than any other feature, that endows Yosemite, especially its wondrous valley, with its mystical allure. From thundering waterfalls, several of them among the world's highest, to sparkling lakes, from rollicking torrents to quiescent pools, water emphatically punctuates Yosemite's predominantly granite land base. Indeed, water in its liquid and solid forms is the primary agent that fashioned and still shapes Yosemite's scenery. As crustal plate movements and intense pressures within the Earth intermittently uplifted the Sierra Nevada along a fault zone on the mountain range's eastern edge, its tilt toward the west progressively steepened. Rivulets flowing into streams that converged into rivers gradually knifed into the rock to engrave a dendroid pattern of drainage channels into a rolling landscape. Then, as the range continued to rise and the gradient increased, master streams such as the Merced River deepened their canyons more rapidly, slicing pathways for Ice Age glaciers.

JEFF GNASS

Although Yosemite Valley's alluvial floor is relatively flat, sloping sections quicken the flow of the Wild and Scenic Merced River that meanders through it. Spawned partially on 13,114-foot Mt. Lyell, Yosemite's highest peak, "The River of Our Lady of Mercy" (translated from the original Spanish name) drains a large watershed. It tumbles from the Sierra crest through steep-sided canyons and past the valley's exalted landmarks to dammed Lake McClure west of the park.

Runoff from snowmelt in the Sierra climaxes in April and May, swelling streams to torrential proportions and waterfalls to roaring cataracts. The fresh spring foliage of white alder, black cottonwood, bigleaf maple, and western azalea brightens the banks of the Merced River. Riparian (streamside) plants play a critical role in stabilizing riverbank soils against the onslaught of rushing water; where human foot traffic denudes banks, soil erosion may become excessive.

Glaciers—Ice on the Move

ED COOPER

JEFF GNASS

Commencing about 2 million years ago, when the climate turned colder, moving ice fields called glaciers crept downslope from the Sierra crest in at least three, probably more, episodes. Quarrying and scraping the land, fingers of debris-laden ice advanced across the rock and, like sandpaper, abraded it, leaving glacial polish and striations as evidence of their tracks when they retreated.

At Olmsted Point, named for Frederick Law Olmsted, designer of New York City's Central Park as well as first chairman of the Yosemite Park Commission (1864-1866), randomly strewn boulders seemingly sprinkled over the scoured bedrock offer convincing testimony for the power of moving ice. Captured and transported from source points between here and the Sierra crest, these glacial erratics were deposited when the last ice sheet melted. Half Dome looks oddly different from this Tioga Road vista.

Overridden by at least one and perhaps several thick glaciers, Liberty Cap (right) an Mt. Broderick (center) exhibit the asymmetric shape of roche moutonnée. *Ice lumbered smoothly over the solid upstream incline of each knob and plucked away granite blockson the jointed (fractured) lee side, steepening and roughening its surface. The "back" side of Half dome overshadows both peaks.*

Although glaciers assaulted Royal Arches and North Dome on the north wall of Yosemite Valley, it is chiefly exfoliation that accounts for their curvature. Sheet joints essentially parallel to the surface topography create layered shells that slowly weather, disintegrate, and spall off, thus rounding angular landforms.

Half Dome

Where did the other half go?

Recognized universally as Yosemite's hallmark, Half Dome stands 4,800 feet above the eastern end of Yosemite Valley. The Ahwahneechee, the indian people who lived in the valley, called it Tis-sa-ack, a woman turned to stone because of her anger; her tears of sadness are still visible on her light-colored face on the sheet wall. Half Dome never really had another "half." In fact, most of the formation is still intact. Although glacial ice did not reach the upper 900 feet of the dome, glaciers undermined its vertically jointed northwest side and frost-wedging pried off the overhead rock.

ED COOPER

Sunset suffuses "Tis-sa-ack" in alpenglow, accentuating its textures and patterns. The 2,000-foot face hosts both rock climbers and nesting peregrine falcons.

Cables allow hikers to climb the 45-degree northeast slope to the summit of Half Dome.

Yosemite Falls...

Yosemite Falls, the worlds fifth highest waterfall at 2,425 feet in total height hits its percussive crescendo when stream runoff peaks in late spring, the beneficiary of melting snow. The Upper Fall plunges 1,430 feet in a single drop. Draining a watershed of largely bare, nonabsorbent granite, Yosemite Creek joins the Merced River in Yosemite Valley. Rock that spalled off the cliff above the cleft to the left of Upper Fall in 1980 covered about a mile of the falls trail.

RUSS FINLEY

RAY ATKESON

The camera lens and photographic angle distort the relative heights of Upper and Lower Yosemite Falls from the short trail to their base. Separated from the Upper Fall by the Middle Cascades (675 feet), the Lower Fall (320 feet) is less than one-forth its senior partner's height—yet twice that of Niagara Falls's.

In the Four Seasons

RAYE SANTOS

By late summer, when little snow remains in the high country, Yosemite Falls has dwindled to a trickle—or dried up completely. Countless episodes of frost-wedging gradually loosened layers of granite that fell away from the cliff to the left of the Upper Fall in 1975; additional rockfall enlarged the light gray patch the following year.

RUSS FINLEY

Occasional snowfall adds a dimension of fantasy and quietude to the valley and its features. Snow and frozen mist cling to the cliff before melting or breaking off as the day warms. Much heavier snowfall higher in the watershed will feed Yosemite Falls the following spring and summer.

El Capitan—Truly a Rock of the Ages

El Capitan–"the chief"–symbolizes strength and durability. Posing imperially at Yosemite Valley's west gates, its summit about 3,600 feet above the valley floor, the massive, solid "El Cap" resisted the grinding, gouging force of glaciers. Endangered peregrine falcons reappeared in Yosemite in 1978 after an absence of many years, their population threatened by pesticides. They now nest on the North American wall (the east face), recognizable by the darker, fine-grained diorite shaped roughly like this continent. A program of "nest augmentation" is aiding their recovery. The large overhang near "Central America" shelters an 80-foot ponderosa pine. Rock climbers ascend this monumental cliff via many routes.

ED COOPER

MONSERRATE J. SCWARTZ

Waterfalls—Yosemite's Signature

Waterfalls are Yosemite's signature. Plummeting from hanging valleys high above trunk canyons such as Yosemite Valley or bouncing down precipitous slopes over boulders and ledges, they put the exclamation point on this landscape where nature makes an eloquent declaration of beauty and power. Perhaps nowhere is the raw power of a tempestuous river more forcefully displayed than at the brink of Nevada Fall, where the Merced River funnels through a narrow chute to plunge 594 feet in a snowy, frothy plume over the upper step of the Giant Stairway. Like its downstream neighbor Vernal Fall, Nevada runs year-round, fed by snowfields and glacial remnants in the upper Merced River basin. A misstep on wet rock or entering the current upstream of the fall has an almost inevitably fatal outcome.

DIANNE DIETRICH LEIS

...falling
twisting
diving
cascading
...creating.

RAY ATKESON

A transitory stream on the eastern buttress of El Capitan, Horsetail Fall flows in late winter and early spring. Not uncommonly, swirling wind on the cliff face joins forces with late-afternoon sunlight to enhance its filmy, ethereal quality.

GAIL BANDINI

*F*ed by the snows of the High Sierra, Yosemite Falls varies throughout the season from a torrential outpouring to a gentle trickle.

Fire–A Force of Nature

Fire has been integral to Sierra Nevada ecosystems for thousands of years. Sparked by lighting, intermittent fires cleansed forests, thinning out understory plants and reducing fuels, opening the canopy to sunlight, fostering diverse regrowth and enhancing conditions for wildlife, cultivating a seedbed, recycling nutrients into the soil, and inhibiting forest pathogens. Most were slow-burning ground fires; occasionally, under extreme conditions, hot fires scorched the land. In the early 1970s, after years of total fire suppression, the National Park Service acknowledged the ecological role of fire, establishing prescribed burning (deliberately set management fires) and prescribed natural fire programs.

NPS PHOTO BY MICHAEL DIXON

At Yosemite's higher elevations, where cooler, moister conditions normally prevail and vegetation is sparser, natural fires are generally monitored and allowed to run their course. Fires that threaten to burn out of control are contained or suppressed, as are all human-caused fires and low-elevation natural fires. Discretion and professional judgement are crucial in fire management.

On August 7, 1990, lightning strikes on steep, low-elevation slopes just inside the park's western boundary ignited fires in dense, dry growth. Firefighters were dispatched immediately, but strong winds spread the blazes quickly, outpacing the crews' ability to hold them in check. The fires burned about 26,000 acres, leaving a mosaic of totally and partially burned, as well as untouched, vegetation.

NPS PHOTO BY DENISE GUIDI

Within several weeks of the 1990 fires, new life was sprouting, even in intensely burned areas. Rebirth and renewal were under way. Over the next 10 to 20 years natural regeneration will flourish, transforming apparent devastation to luxuriant gardens of rich biological diversity. Fire is not so much a force of destruction as it is agent of change, the one constant in nature.

NPS PHOTO BY DENISE GUIDI

The *Moods* of *the* *Valley*

ED COOPER

Standing apart from the south wall of the valley, the product of exfoliation and frost-splitting of vertically jointed granite, one of two Cathedral Spires pierces a typically deep-blue Sierran sky. The resemblance to a church steeple is obvious!

RUSS FINLEY

Morning light and an unruffled Merced River accent the Three Brothers, which symbolize the sons of Tenaya, the last chief of the Ahwahneechee. Eagle Peak, its apex never glaciated, represents the eldest son. Parallel master joints, or fracture planes, account for the uniform angle of the westward-tilting slopes. Like a rampart, this otherwise-solid mass defied the plowing, gouging incursions of glaciers in their Ice Age encounters.

GAIL BANDINI

All of the water from Yosemite Valley and the surrounding areas comes together to form the Merced River. The flow varies from season to season, from placid to turbulent. It shows us both the beauty and power of water.

Overleaf: Tenaya Lake glistens in its glacially gouged basin. Photo by Jeff Gnass.

CARR CLIFTON

The High Sierra Country

If the valley is the heart of Yosemite, the high country is its soul. "Thousands of tired, nerve-shaken, over-civilized people are beginning to find out that going to the mountains is going home; that wildness is a necessity; and that mountain parks and reservations are useful not only as fountains of timber and irrigating rivers, but as fountains of life."

Written in 1898, John Muir's words are no less fitting today. Reaching summits more than 13,000 feet in elevation on the Sierra crest, most of it formally designated as wilderness in 1984, the high country of Muir's "Range of Light" beckons hikers and backpackers to sample his "measureless mountain days" on 800 miles of park trails.

Spring arrives late in the high country. After a "normal" winter, snow lingers in Dana Meadows, at almost 10,000 feet in elevation, and on Mammoth Peak well after the Tioga Road opens for the season, usually in late May. "Suncups" pock the surface.

The Tuolumne Meadows –
John Muir's Country

*In Tuolumne
Meadows, at 8,600
feet the Sierra's
largest subalpine
meadow, standing
water from recent
snowmelt mirrors
the unglaciated
summits of Unicorn
Peak (center) and
the Cockscomb.
Wet meadows are
especially fragile
and vulnerable
to impacts.*

ED COOPER

The deeply weathered granite on Medlicott Dome above Lower Cathedral Lake suggest glaciation was insufficient to smooth the irregular surface. Fine-grained feldspar crystals armor the humps, confirming the relative resistance of different minerals to wind and water. The summit of Tresidder Peak, named for the long-time president of the Yosemite Park and Curry Co., escaped glacial ice.

Life in the Harsh Sierra

JOHN DITTLI

Inhabiting rockslides, the wary, reclusive pika, a relative of rabbits, dries and stores herbaceous plants to sustain itself over the long high-country winter under deep snow.

BOB RONEY

Preferring streamsides, the adaptable Pacific treefrog, shown nestled in an aster, ranges from the Central Valley of California to near treeline.

The succulent, fleshy leaves of stonecrop store water, an adaptation to the intense summer sunlight and desiccating winds of high, rocky slopes. Survival under these harsh conditions, where moisture is precious, demands water conservation.

...life is found in all the strangest places

PAT O'HARA

BOB RONEY

The blood-red saprophytic snow plant emerges from the forest floor soon after the snow melts.

Cradled in the shadow of aptly named Ragged Peak, its stark summit crag untouched by glacial ice, the three Young Lakes, in bowl-like cirques at about 9,900 feet in elevation, embody the bold, yet serene, essence of alpine wilderness. Weathering along vertical joints has flaked the mountain's granite and sharpened its toothy spire. Lupines add contrasting color to the lower lake's shoreline.

"*Fretting the air into music*," in the words of John Muir, the "tuneful and joyful" Tuolumne River cascades down California Falls in symphonic extravagance. Proclaimed a Wild and Scenic River in 1984, the Tuolumne drains the northern half of the park. Cloud-seeding over the watershed, started in 1990 by San Joaquin Valley water interests, will adversely affect ecological patterns and relationships.

LARRY ULRICH

The namesake dome of early Tuolumne Meadows settler and goatherd John Baptist Lembert is a classic roche moutonnée (sheep's back)—smoothly sloped on the glacial upstream side and steeply jagged downstream.

ED COOPER

31

GAIL BANDINI

From its origins along the Sierra crest, the Tuolumne River merges countless tributaries into a vibrant artery that courses through the deeply gorged Grand Canyon of the Tuolumne and leads backpackers to Hetch Hetchy.

CHARLIE BORLAND

"Dam Hetch Hetchy!" Muir wrote. "As well dam for water-tanks the people's cathedrals and churches, for no holier temple has ever been consecrated by the heart of man." Its similarity to Yosemite Valley is striking—a glaciated canyon, waterfalls (Wapama Falls, center), domes, even a near-facsimile of El Capitan and nesting peregrine falcons. Its name is derived from a Miwok word for a native grass. A recent controversial proposal to drain and restore Hetch Hetchy died, lacking adequate political support.

Kolana Rock soars above bathtub-ringed Hetch Hetchy Reservoir. O'Shaughnessy Dam, authorized by the Raker Act in 1913, completed in 1923, and heightened in the 1930s, impounded the Tuolumne River—within the already-established park—and inundated a saddened Muir's "other Yosemite" to supply water and power to San Francisco.

FRED HIRSCHMANN

ED COOPER

The meaning of Tueeulala Falls's name, like Wapama's, is unknown. Fleeting and appearing delicate, the spray drops about 1,000 feet from the cliff's prow until the stream dries in mid-summer.

Big Trees – the Largest Living Things on Earth

Virtually every possible superlative has probably been bestowed on the giant sequoia, also called Big Tree and Sierra redwood. Notable for its longevity, some reaching close to 3,000 years of age, and its height—some specimens surpass 30-story buildings—*Sequoiadendron giganteum* is neither the oldest living thing nor the tallest. Rather, it is the behemoth's colossal size that inspires reverence and wonder—even disbelief.

In sheer volume it is the world's largest lifeform. Once more widely distributed, naturally seeded giant sequoias are now confined to 75 isolated groves on the Sierra Nevada's western flank. Most of the groves, having escaped nineteenth-century logging, are now protected. Three lie within Yosemite's boundaries.

The Mariposa Grove, a legacy of the Yosemite Grant located near the park's south entrance, is the largest and most accessible. The big trees of either the Merced or Tuolumne grove were probably the first seen by non-Indian people, members of the Joseph Walker party who crossed the Sierra in 1833.

A mature sequoia may annually produce 2,000 cones that cling, tightly closed, to the branches for years until a feeding chickaree (Douglas squirrel), a tiny boring beetle, or the heat of a fire dries the cones, thus releasing the seeds that resemble oat flakes. In fact, a regime of occasional fires is vital to sequoia reproduction.

To survive, sequoias must be vigorous and tenacious. Even in death they persist. The wood, though brittle, resists decay, and relics remain on the ground for centuries.

GAIL BANDINI

The massive butt swell of a sequoia magnifies the sense of feeling dwarfed. The tree's root system, spreading 100-150 feet around the base only 2 to 5 feet beneath the surface, is vulnerable to excessive trampling, which compacts and erodes soil.

...with **giants feet**, they **march slowly** into **eternity**...

Enshrouded by fog that enhances the grove's cathedral-like atmosphere, the Grizzly Giant, about 2,700 years old, may be the oldest living big tree. Topped repeatedly by lightning and scarred by countless fires, the mammoth trunk stands "only" 209 feet tall but is almost 31 feet across at its base. The large elbowed branch 95 feet up the trunk is 6 feet in diameter.

ED COOPER

GRIZZLY GIANT

Land of Many Trees

A robust tree, the western juniper attains exceptional girth in relation to its height. Growing sparsely on domes and crags, in rock crevices rather than a soil substrate, gnarled junipers tolerate austerities that other confiners cannot survive. Exposed to blistering winds and blizzards, generous snowfall, intense sunlight, and dry summers, they may reach an age of 3,000 years! Birds play a crucial role in dispersing their seeds.

JEFF GNASS

With roundish leaves that quiver in even a light breeze, thin-barked quaking aspens dapple the high country with splashes of gold in the fall. The only deciduous tree in the subalpine forest, sun-loving aspens grow in clonal groves, sprouting chiefly from single root systems rather than seeds.

CHUCK PLACE

ED COOPER

The lovely spring blossoms of the moisture-loving Pacific dogwood, its deciduous leaves not fully developed, and the reddish, creased bark of a staunch incense-cedar– not a true cedar–adorn the banks of the brimming Merced River in Yosemite Valley. Both shade-tolerant and abundant, the two species share a common range at low middle elevations. The dogwood's prominent bracts—not petals—embrace the inconspicuous central flowers that ripen in the fall into succulent crimson fruits favored by birds.

People at Yosemite

Preserve or playground? Wilderness or resort? Recreation or re-creation? Ask a random sampling of the 4.1 million people who now visit the park each year what the Yosemite experience should be, and the answers reflect diverse perceptions and values. To some Yosemite is a hallowed sanctuary; to others a recreational mecca; to many a magical, variable blend of active discovery and passive interaction. By almost anyone's yardstick, though, it is special. Native people first inhabited this setting well over 4,000 years ago, living in tune with the land. The arrival of non-Indian people in the mid-nineteenth century forever changed their lifeways—and the destiny of Yosemite itself. Explorers and trappers came first, then miners and settlers. After the Mariposa Battalion's incursion into Yosemite Valley in 1851, word spread about the valley's stupendous scenery. In 1855 the first tourist parties entered the valley, and settlers and entrepreneurs soon followed. The tales of incredible splendor attracted artists, photographers, writers, and promoters who extolled Yosemite's grandeur. Hotels and homesteads sprouted, and visitation blossomed. So did efforts to preserve its beauty. The landmark Yosemite Grant in 1864, the genesis of the park movement, set aside Yosemite Valley and the Mariposa Grove to be administered by the State of California for "...public use, resort and recreation." On October 1, 1890, Congress designated Yosemite as "reserved forest lands," making it the nation's third-oldest national park. Over the ensuing century, park managers have continually grappled with the dilemma of balancing visitor use with resource preservation.

Spray churned up by Vernal Fall in spring and early summer drenches both hikers and the luxuriant vegetation on the popular Mist Trail, a 1.5-mile walk from the valley floor to the top. Even a short stroll away from the trappings of civilization kindles a closer personal connection with the intrinsic rhythms of nature. GARY LADD

Seeing, feeling, being—the most personal Yosemite encounter. Standing on the footbridge below Lower Yosemite Fall, immersed in its baptism, watch the prismatic play of light in its spray. On a spring night, under a full moon, revel in its "moonbow." Listen to its bellowing roar. With "Nature streaming into us" (John Muir), let your sense of wonder soar, and feel your kinship with the Earth.

DICK DIETRICH

Riding on a paved bikeway obscured here by meadow grass, bicyclist enjoy exercise and a delightful way to experience the valley. Bicycles afford alternative transportation that relieves traffic congestion in the valley on busy days, but off surfaced routes they denude vegetation and create unsightly scars in meadows and woodlands.

DENNIS FLAHERTY

Day's early light unveils a crystalline cloak of frost on corn lilies and grasses in high, moist meadows beyond the valley's rims. The corn lilies' curled leaves, still wrapped around unseen stems that may grow to six feet in height, indicate late spring or early summer.

The baronial Ahwahnee Hotel opened in 1927 in Yosemite Valley. Constructed of native stone and wood, the Ahwahnee (the Miwok name for the valley, meaning "place of the gaping mouth") was built at the direction of National Park Service Director Stephen Mather as a luxury accommodation for wealthy guests.

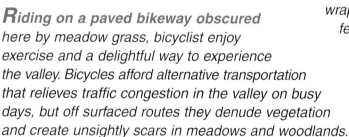

GAIL BANDINI

...where the rocks breathe, we find there our solace

ED COOPER

Using the technical gear needed for safety and support, rock climbers painstakingly and methodically scale the near-vertical northwest face of Half Dome. Since the pioneering ascent in 1957, the 2,000-foot wall has challenged skilled climbers to chart a number of routes. As climbing has grown in popularity, impacts on cliffs have increased. "Clean" climbing techniques developed in recent years greatly reduce damage to rocks. The Yosemite Mountaineering School offers professional climbing instruction.

DICK DIETRICH

Serendipitous encounters, often simple and sometimes close, are exciting moments. Stay alert and attuned to your surroundings. When nature crosses your path, don't miss it.

Ranger-led interpretive activities add a dimension of understanding, discovery, and enrichment to a park experience. Professionally conducted walks such as the short Sentinel Dome hike, evening talks, and cultural programs emphasize resource values, park use ethics, and stewardship.

DIANNE DIETRICH LEIS

A lavish winter panorama of Yosemite Valley and the High Sierra wilderness spreads out a visual and emotional feast for a cross-country skier at Dewey Point, located across the valley from El Capitan. Snow buffers noise, amplifying the sounds of silence, and protects life beneath its blanket of insulation.

FRANK S. BALTHIS

The use of horses is traditional in western national parks, predating the parks themselves. Other than the flat-brimmed hat, nothing seems more symbolic of the National Park Service than a ranger on horseback. Well-trained horses tolerant of people can take patrol rangers to places where vehicles can't—at a faster pace than a person on foot.

RAYE SANTOS

FRED HIRSCHMANN

Built in 1879 near the base of the Four-Mile Trail, the picturesque Yosemite Chapel is the site of regularly scheduled worship services and numerous weddings. Relocated to the Old Village in 1901, the structure is the park's second-oldest building in continuous use.

SUGGESTED READING

ARNO, STEPHEN F., et. al. *Discovering Sierra Trees* (also *Birds, Mammals,* and *Reptiles and Amphibians).* Three Rivers and Yosemite, California: Sequoia Natural History Association and Yosemite Association, 1974-1985.

HUBER, N. KING. *The Geologic Story of Yosemite National Park.* Yosemite, California: Yosemite Association, 1989; reprint of U.S. Geological Survey Bulletin 1595, U.S. Government Printing Office, Washington, D.C., 1987.

JONES, WILLIAM R. *Yosemite: The Story Behind the Scenery.* Las Vegas, Nevada: KC Publications, Inc., 1989 (revised edition).

MEDLEY, STEVEN P. *The Complete Guidebook to Yosemite National Park.* Yosemite, California: Yosemite Association, 1996 (revised edition).

NATIONAL PARK SERVICE. *Yosemite: Official National Park Handbook.* Washington, D.C.: U.S. Government Printing Office, 1990.

STETSON, LEE. *The Wild Muir - Twenty-two of John Muir's Greatest Adventures.* Yosemite, California: Yosemite Association, 1994.

Note: Any book written by John Muir is recommended.

All About Yosemite National Park

Yosemite Association

The Yosemite Association is a nonprofit organization dedicated to the support of Yosemite National Park through a program of visitor services, publications, and membership activities. The association was founded in 1923 as the Yosemite Natural History Association.

From membership fees, donations, and the publication and sale of literature and interpretive items, the association currently provides over $300,000 annually to the park's visitor information, educational, and interpretive programs. It also organizes volunteers to work on meadow, trail, and other much-needed park restoration projects. It conducts over 60 outdoor classes on natural history, Native American lifeways, art, and photography. Finally, the association operates and/or sponsors the Ostrander Ski Hut, Art Activity Center, and other valuable programs.

Association members receive discounts at its book outlets and on most of its outdoor adventures, get a quarterly journal, are invited to special events, and have the satisfaction of supporting Yosemite. To enroll, contact the Yosemite Association, P.O. Box 230, El Portal, CA 95318; phone: (209) 379-2646; web: www.yosemite.org.

PIKA
BY JOHN DITTLI

The Yosemite Fund

The Yosemite Fund is also a nonprofit organization. It raises money from Yosemite enthusiasts to protect and restore the park and enhance visitors' experiences. Dating from 1988, in its first 13 years the fund distributed over $13 million for more than 150 projects. These included installation of 2,000 bear-proof food lockers, rehabilitation of Cook's Meadow in the heart of Yosemite Valley, trail rebuilding, and a park visitor orientation film.

Fund members are Friends of Yosemite and donors of $25 or more receive a gift for joining, the biannual magazine Approach *featuring articles on the park, and acknowledgement at the Friends of Yosemite Honor Wall at the Valley Visitor Center.*

To become a Friend of Yosemite, contact The Yosemite Fund, P.O. Box 637, Yosemite, CA 95389; phone: (800) 4MY-PARK; web: www.yosemitefund.org.

The Yosemite Institute

The Yosemite Institute is a private nonprofit organization dedicated to providing educational adventures in nature's classroom to inspire a personal connection to the natural world and responsible actions to sustain it.

For over 30 years, Yosemite National Institutes has served over 40,000 youth and adults annually through a unique variety of environmental education programs at our national park campuses in California and Washington.

Contact Yosemite National Institute, P.O. Box 487, Yosemite, CA 95389; phone: (209) 379-9511; fax: (209) 379-9510; web: www.yni.org.

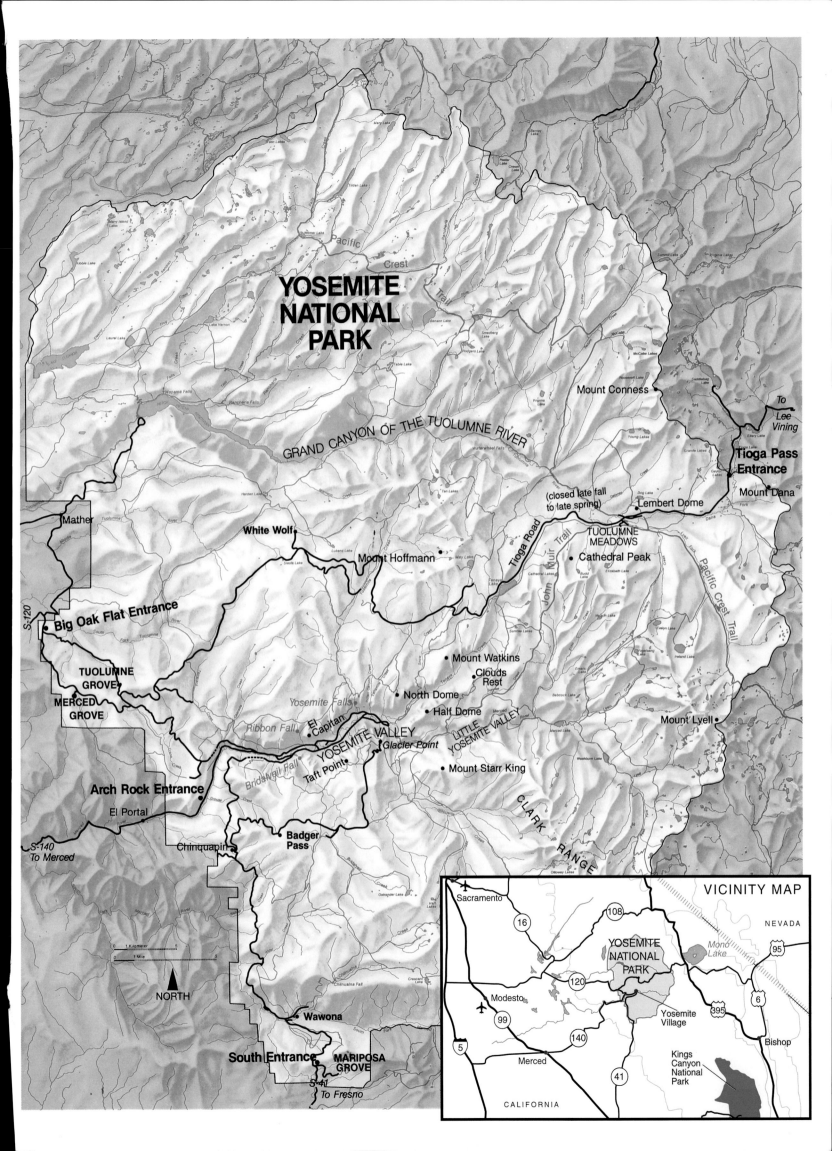